THE FACTS ABOUT
Diabetes

Claire Llewellyn

Thameside Press

Distributed in the United States by
Smart Apple Media
1980 Lookout Drive
North Mankato, MN 56003

Text by Claire Llewellyn
Illustrations by Tom Connell

Editor: Russell McLean
Designer: Helen James
Picture researcher: Frances Vargo
Medical consultant: Jill Humphries, community children's nurse, Welwyn Garden City, England

Thanks to Gary Feit, Juvenile Diabetes Research Foundation International, and Laura Vazquez,
American Diabetes Association, for help with the U.S. edition.

Printed in China

9 8 7 6 5 4 3 2 1

Library of Congress Cataloging-in-Publication Data

Llewellyn, Claire.
    Diabetes / written by Claire Llewellyn.
       p. cm. -- (The facts about ...)
    Includes index.
    ISBN 1-929298-97-8
       1. Diabetes--Juvenile literature. 2. Diabetes in children--Juvenile literature. [1. Diabetes.
    2. Diseases.] I. Title. II. Facts about (Mankato, Minn.)

    RC660.5 .L565 2001
    616.4'62--dc21

                                                            2001023423

Picture acknowledgements:
John Birdsall Photography: 20b. Corbis: Jenny Woodcock/Reflections Photolibrary 25t. James
Davis Photography: 12. Diabetes UK: 5t. Eye Ubiquitous: Bob Battersby 5b; Peter Blake 26b;
Bennett Dean cover bl, 21t, 22b; Mostyn 3r, 6b; Yiorgos Nikiteas 27t; Paul Seheult 13b, 16b;
Skjold 25b. Sally & Richard Greenhill: Sally Greenhill 17b, 26t, 28t. Photofusion: B. Apicella
13t; Janis Austin cover background, 4b; Richard Eaton 19b; Ute Klaphake 29b; Christa Stadtler
18t, 20t; Bob Watkins 9b. Rex Features: Woman's Weekly 21b; Mark Lloyd 23b; John Moran
22t; Today/Gooch/Levenson 23t; Zoom/D.P.P.I. 3b, 27b. Science Photo Library: Scott Camazine/
Sue Trainor 11l; CC Studio 8b, 18b; Mark Clarke cover br, 3c, 4t, 10t, 16t, 29t; Gable/Jerrican
24t; James Holmes/Celltech Ltd 28b; St Bartholomew's Hospital 19t; Saturn Stills 11r, 14, 24b.
Telegraph Colour Library: Hugh Burden 1, 17t; Tipp Howell cover bc, 8t; Antonia Reeve 9t;
Paul Windsor 7. David Towersey: 15.

Contents

Words in **bold** are explained
in the glossary on page 30

What is diabetes?

Diabetes is a serious condition that affects the way the body uses sugar. Someone with diabetes has too much sugar in their blood. They need treatment for this all their life.

The signs of diabetes
You cannot tell from just looking if someone has diabetes, but you can tell from what they have to do. Many people with diabetes need to give themselves injections.

You can't tell just by looking whether someone has diabetes.

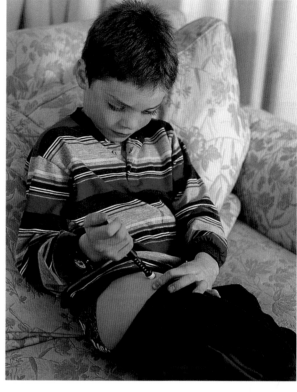

Children with diabetes have to learn to give themselves injections.

The right amount of sugar
The injections give the body an important substance called **insulin** (see pages 6–7). This controls the amount of sugar in the blood. People with diabetes also need to think carefully about which foods they eat and when. This helps to make sure they get the right amount of sugar all through the day and night.

Damage to the body

People with diabetes can never forget their condition, as it needs to be carefully controlled at all times. If it is not treated, diabetes causes tiredness and weight loss, and damages parts of the body such as the heart, **kidneys**, eyes, and feet. This can be very dangerous.

Diabetes is a condition that affects both young and old.

Living with diabetes

Many people have to live with diabetes. This is how some of them describe what it is like:

"I need to watch what I eat."

"I have to inject myself every day."

"I need to eat snacks all the time."

"I'm always testing my blood."

"I get tired and shaky sometimes."

People with diabetes need to think about which foods they eat and when.

What happens inside?

Our bodies use the sugar in blood as fuel. If a person has diabetes, their body is unable to use sugar because they are missing an important substance called insulin.

From food to fuel

When we eat, our food is broken down into different forms that the body can use. One group of foods, known as **carbohydrates**, are turned into a sugar called **glucose**, which quickly enters the **bloodstream**.

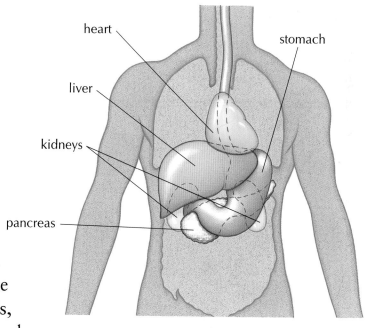

heart
stomach
liver
kidneys
pancreas

Insulin is made by special cells inside the pancreas. This is a long, thin gland behind the stomach.

As soon as the amount of sugar in the blood begins to rise, a **gland** called the **pancreas** begins to make insulin. Its job is to help the sugar enter the body's **cells**, which then use it as fuel. As we burn this fuel—by working, playing, and being alive— our sugar levels begin to fall. When this happens, the pancreas stops producing insulin until sugar levels in the blood rise again.

Pasta is one kind of carbohydrate.

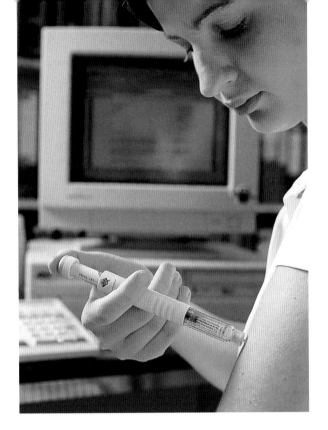

Insulin injections help people with diabetes to keep their blood sugar levels normal.

The trouble with diabetes

When someone has diabetes, glucose enters the bloodstream but cannot get into the body's cells. This is because the pancreas does not work properly and cannot produce insulin. So the sugar stays in the bloodstream. The level rises higher and higher. Eventually there is so much sugar in the blood that it overflows into the person's **urine**.

Did you know?

- Diabetes mellitus is the full name for diabetes. It comes from the Greek for "fountain of honey." This describes the sweet-smelling urine of someone with diabetes.
- People with diabetes may have a blood sugar level that is up to ten times higher than normal.
- Carbohydrates are divided into sugary foods, such as cakes and cookies, and **starchy** foods such as bread, **tortillas**, **plantain**, potatoes, pasta, cereals, and rice.

What happens next?

When extra sugar leaks into their urine, a person needs to urinate, or pee, a lot. They need to drink lots of water to make up the lost fluids. More importantly, a person with diabetes does not make fuel from their food. They feel tired and start to lose weight.

Solving the problem

People with diabetes need to give their body the insulin it cannot make itself. They do this by giving themselves injections of insulin every day. Injected insulin does the same job as insulin made by the body, helping glucose to enter the cells, and keeping sugar levels normal.

Types of diabetes

There are two types of diabetes. Children and young people usually have one type, while older people have the other. Both types of diabetes are caused by a lack of insulin, but are treated in different ways.

Type 1 diabetes

The kind of diabetes that most often affects children and young people is known as type 1. In type 1 diabetes, the pancreas cannot make insulin. Doctors do not know why this happens, but there are a number of possible reasons (see pages 12–13).

A strong thirst is an important early symptom of diabetes.

Type 1 diabetes develops very quickly, in some cases over just a few weeks. The **symptoms** can be severe, but fortunately the condition is easily **diagnosed**. There is no known cure for type 1, but it can be controlled quickly with injections of insulin, a healthy diet, and exercise.

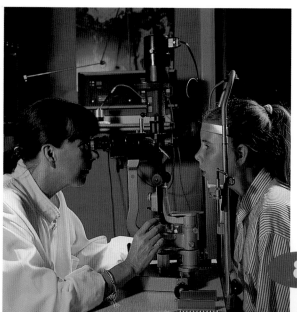

An optician may be the first person to notice that someone has diabetes because the condition causes changes to the eyes.

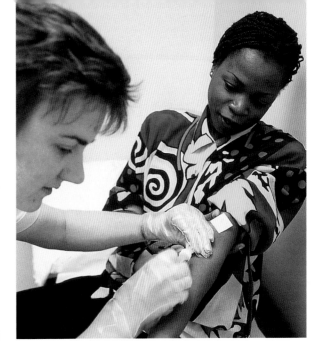

Symptoms of diabetes

- A strong thirst and a dry mouth.
- Endless trips to the bathroom.
- Lack of energy and tiredness.
- Blurred vision.
- Weight loss.

Diabetes is easily diagnosed with a simple blood test.

Type 2 diabetes

Type 2 diabetes usually affects people over 40. The pancreas makes some insulin, but not enough for the body's needs. People with type 2 may be overweight or eating the wrong sort of food. The condition develops slowly and the symptoms are usually less severe than in type 1. People with type 2 do not usually need to inject insulin. They take tablets to make the pancreas work harder and may need to change to a healthier diet.

Diagnosing diabetes

Diabetes is diagnosed by testing the sugar levels in blood and urine samples. Diabetes is confirmed if the levels are very high. People may be diagnosed by their doctor or in a hospital center. They may then see a specialist **diabetologist** and a diabetes educator.

Type 2 diabetes usually develops later in life.

Did you know?

- People with undiagnosed diabetes are incredibly thirsty. Young children have even been found drinking from ponds.
- In the past, doctors diagnosed diabetes by tasting a person's urine to see if it was sweet!

Injecting insulin

Young people with diabetes need to have regular injections of insulin. Giving yourself injections or giving them to children sounds scary. But diabetes has to be treated this way.

Giving an injection
Giving injections is something most people would find a challenge. But people with diabetes cannot take insulin in a tablet because it is destroyed by juices in the stomach.

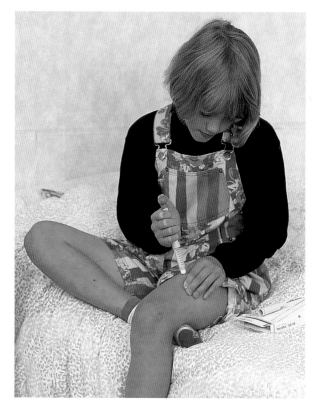

Injecting can be tricky at first, but it becomes much easier with practice.

Most people inject themselves two to four times a day with a tool called an insulin pen. Some people use a **syringe**.

Where to inject?
The best places to inject are in the fatty parts of the body. It is important to change injection sites regularly or the skin may become lumpy and sore.

Where to inject insulin

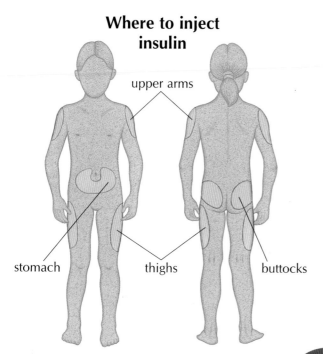

upper arms

stomach   thighs   buttocks

All about insulin

People who are just starting to use insulin are given a recommended starting **dose**. As they become more experienced they can use more or less insulin, according to their blood sugar level (see pages 14–15). Supplies of insulin last for two to three years if they are stored in the fridge. Injecting cold insulin is painful, though, so it should be left out to reach room temperature first.

How to inject with an insulin pen

1 Wash your hands and make sure that the injection site is clean.
2 Dial up the units for your insulin dose.
3 Pinch a fold of skin between your thumb and finger and push the needle into the skin.
4 Put your thumb on top of the plunger and inject all the insulin.
5 Count to five. Take the needle out slowly, keeping it straight.

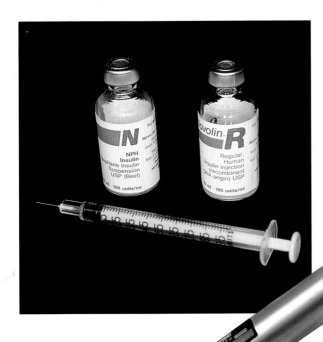

People with diabetes soon become used to handling a syringe (above) or an insulin pen (right).

"I did my first injection in hospital, two days after I was diagnosed. The nurse showed me what to do and I practiced on an orange first. Then, I just stuck the needle in myself. Five minutes later I was in tears. Not because it hurt particularly, but because it had dawned on me that I'd be having injections for the rest of my life."

KATY LOUISE, AGE 17

Who gets diabetes?

Diabetes can affect anyone from newborn babies to the very old. Coping with it can be a challenge at any age.

The causes of diabetes

Doctors do not know why some people get diabetes and others do not, but there are several possible reasons. Diabetes seems to run in families, although it is hard to predict who will develop it. In some people, the condition is caused by damage to the pancreas after an infection or illness. Diet and stress may also play a part.

Did you know?

- Nearly 16 million people (almost 6 per cent of the U.S. population) have diabetes. About a third of these people do not know they have it.
- Type 2 accounts for 90–95 per cent of diabetes in the U.S.
- You cannot catch diabetes from somebody else.
- Eating candies or the wrong foods does not cause diabetes.
- Smoking is especially harmful if you have diabetes.

Young children

Diabetes in very young children has to be managed by their parents. They need to learn to give injections, test blood glucose (see pages 14–15), and think carefully about their children's eating habits. Many parents are anxious if their child is a fussy eater and worry about hurting them with an injection.

Several members of the same family may have diabetes.

Foot care

Diabetes can narrow the **blood vessels** so that less blood reaches the feet. Even small infections can be very slow to heal, so it's important to look after your feet.

1 Check your feet daily for cuts or blisters.
2 Wash your feet daily and dry them well. Rub cream into the skin if it is dry.
3 Keep your feet warm.
4 Always wear well-fitting shoes.

People with diabetes often have cold feet. Wearing thick socks or slippers helps keep the feet warm.

Teenagers

Most teenagers can manage their diabetes and handle the injections. But keeping control of the condition means thinking ahead and sticking to regular mealtimes, which becomes more difficult in the teenage years.

Older people

People are much more likely to have diabetes when they are older. They usually have type 2. This means they rarely have to manage injections, but may have to make big changes to their lifestyle—such as giving up smoking, doing more exercise, and eating a healthier diet.

Health problems

High blood sugar levels can harm the body over many years. If people don't control their diabetes, they have more chance of developing health problems in the future. These include **heart attacks**, eye damage, and kidney damage— as well as foot and leg problems.

As children grow older, they find it harder to stick to regular mealtimes.

13

Checking sugar levels

The amount of sugar in our blood changes during the day. If you have diabetes, it is important to be aware of these changes.

To test the level of sugar in blood, first prick the side of a fingertip. Then put a drop of blood on to a blood-testing strip.

Up and down

When we eat or drink, our blood sugar level rises. Later, as glucose enters our cells, the level falls. If we exercise, it falls much faster. For most of us, the pancreas works in step with our blood sugar. When the level is high, it makes enough insulin to bring it down to normal; when it is low, the pancreas makes less insulin so that it doesn't drop any further.

Keeping a balance

People with diabetes have to control their blood sugar levels themselves. This means thinking about the food they eat, the amount of insulin they inject, and the amount of exercise they do. All three things must be kept in balance. The only way to do this is by checking the sugar in their blood. In other words, they test their blood four or five times every day. Blood-testing strips and electronic meters make testing easier.

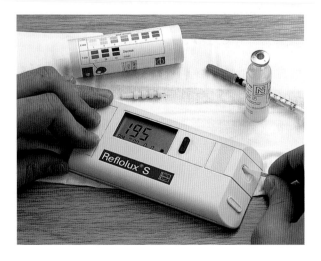

Put the blood-testing strip into an electronic meter to give an instant sugar level reading.

- Before each main meal.
- Before and after exercise.
- Two hours after a meal.
- Before bedtime.
- At night if you are worried about blood sugar levels dropping too low while you sleep.

Always test more if you feel tired or unwell, if you travel abroad, or if your daily routine changes.

Recording results

It is important to record blood test results, either in a diary or a meter's electronic memory. Doctors, nurses, and diabetologists use the results to check that blood sugar levels are being kept within safe limits. Over a period of time, they can see whether the insulin dose is right or needs changing. For example, a teenager growing very fast probably needs a larger dose.

Did you know?

- Fingertips are good places for blood testing because the blood vessels lie near the surface.
- There are fewer nerve endings on the sides of the fingertips. This makes testing less painful.
- Scientists are working on a painless blood test that uses a laser beam.
- People who control their blood sugar well are more likely to avoid future health problems.

Putting the hands in warm water before checking glucose helps the blood to flow more easily.

Highs and lows

People with diabetes find that controlling blood sugar levels is not always easy. Sometimes the sugar level is too low and sometimes it is too high. This may make them feel unwell.

The highs

Having high blood sugar is known as **hyperglycemia**. The symptoms of this are the same as when a person is first diagnosed with diabetes. They are thirsty, keep going to the bathroom, feel tired, and start to lose weight. Hyperglycemia may be caused by infections, by eating too many sugary foods, by not taking enough insulin, or by missing injections. It is important to correct high blood sugar, as it can cause health problems in later life.

Feeling strange and slightly dizzy are often warning signs of hypoglycemia.

The lows

Having low blood sugar is known as **hypoglycemia**. Someone may have this condition for several reasons—such as if they eat later than usual, have an unexpected burst of exercise, or inject too much insulin. Hypoglycemia comes on quickly and there are many warning signs. The person may look pale, feel dizzy, have a headache, or start to sweat.

A child who is feeling too tired to play may have hyperglycemia.

Hypoglycemia can be treated quickly by drinking fruit juice, then eating candy.

Sometimes a person with low blood sugar loses their temper suddenly or finds it hard to concentrate. Most people with diabetes recognize these signs and take steps to raise their blood sugar. But if they don't, then someone else has to do it for them immediately. Without treatment, the person may become **unconscious**.

Treating hypoglycemia

1 Give a fast-acting carbohydrate drink, such as fruit juice, and then a few candies, glucose tablets, or a mini-chocolate bar.
2 When the person starts to feel better, give them a starchy snack, such as a sandwich or some cookies and milk.
3 If the person is unconscious, do not try to feed them. Lie them on their side with their chin tilted up. If they don't recover after a few minutes, call an ambulance (911).

Avoiding low blood sugar

Always carrying a few candies or glucose tablets is a simple way to help avoid lows. Many people with diabetes carry an identity card or bracelet so that they get the right treatment if they become unconscious. After a low, it's important to test that the blood sugar level has returned to normal.

A starchy snack such as a sandwich steadies the body's sugar level after it drops.

The diabetes center

Some peole with diabetes visit a diabetes center. Here, a team of nurses, doctors, diabetologists, diabetes educators, and **dieticians** check the diabetes and give advice and support.

At the center

People with diabetes are given a thorough check-up at the center. Over several visits, a nurse weighs and measures them, looks at their blood-test results, examines their injection sites, checks their injection technique, tests their blood, and makes sure they can manage their diabetes.

Weighing and measuring give a picture of a child's general health.

Most Americans with diabetes are diagnosed by their doctor.

If a regular doctor finds that a person has diabetes, they may be sent to a specialist diabetologist for more treatment. Sometimes, people go to a hospital in an emergency and it is the hospital that discovers the diabetes. Once the diabetes is found, the kidneys, feet, and eyes are checked for other health problems.

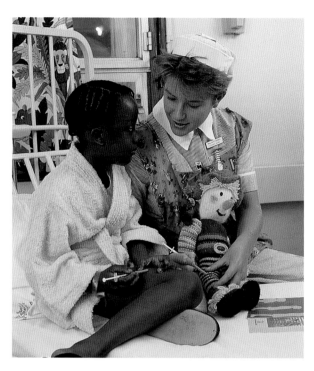

A diabetes educator visits children with diabetes who have to stay in the hospital.

Diabetes educators

A diabetes educator visits parents, schools, and anyone who needs to know more about diabetes. The job of an educator is to inform people about the condition, explain how to deal with low blood sugar, and help them solve any problems. Between visits he or she takes phone calls from parents, answers their questions, and acts as a link between families, schools, doctors, and hospitals. Educators also visit children with diabetes who are in the hospital.

"It's pretty cool having people fussing over you when you're nervous and scared. It might seem like everyone's prodding and poking you, but after all they do know best. After a while it becomes a way of life."

ECHO, AGE 15

A dietician advises people with diabetes about choosing a healthy diet.

Food and drink

For people with diabetes, a healthy diet is especially important to control their condition. They need to eat the right kinds of food, not only at mealtimes but in between, too.

Little and often

People with diabetes need to eat the same healthy diet recommended to everyone. It should be low in fat, sugar, and salt, but high in **fiber** and with plenty of fruit and vegetables.

Fresh fruit and vegetables are important for everyone, and especially for people with diabetes.

It is important for them to eat regularly during the day, as this helps to keep blood sugar levels stable. They may need to eat snacks between mealtimes and before they go to bed.

Important foods

Carbohydrates are important for people with diabetes because these are the foods that put sugar into the blood. Starchy carbohydrates, such as potatoes, rice, bread, tortillas, pasta, and cereal, release sugar slowly. They should be eaten at every meal.

A milky drink before bedtime helps to stop sugar levels dropping too low in the night.

Dieticians

Soon after a person is diagnosed with diabetes, they may have an appointment with the dietician. Dieticians are experts on food and how it affects the body. They provide a basic plan for a healthy diet and offer plenty of advice.

Read the label to find out how much sugar and fat a food contains.

Sugary carbohydrates, such as cakes, jam, ice cream, candies, desserts, soda or pop all release sugar quickly. They can send sugar levels soaring, which is why they are good for treating an attack of low blood sugar. But as a daily food, they need to be eaten more sparingly—before exercise perhaps, or as a treat after a meal.

A slow-acting starchy carbohydrate, such as bread, should be eaten at every meal.

Healthy snacks

People with diabetes need to eat snacks between meals. Snacks can add extra fat to the diet, so it is good to eat low-fat foods such as fresh or dried fruit, toast, yogurt, rice cakes, breadsticks, a cereal bar, or a bowl of cereal and milk.

Did you know?

- Modern low-sugar, low-fat foods are a good choice for people with diabetes.
- People with diabetes should never skip a meal. This could lead to low blood sugar.
- It's a good idea to avoid lots of soda or pop, or replace them with "low-sugar", "diet" substitutes.
- Foods with the label "diabetic" are unnecessary and are no better than ordinary foods.

Sport and exercise

Exercise is important for everyone. It's fun and it keeps you fit. Thousands of people with diabetes enjoy sports, and some become famous champions!

Using energy

When we exercise, we burn energy and use up the glucose in our blood. This can cause problems for people with diabetes. If they use up too much glucose, they risk having low blood sugar. They can avoid this with some simple precautions.

Every activity we do burns energy.

Before exercise

People with diabetes need extra glucose before starting any energetic activity. They need to eat a snack such as a mini-chocolate bar, a cereal bar, or a couple of cookies. If the activity is likely to be long and hard, then they will need to eat even more.

A juicy orange boosts sugar levels half way through a game.

During an activity

During exercise, blood sugar levels start to drop, and a person with diabetes may need some instant sugar. It is important to have some glucose tablets or a sugary drink nearby to give an extra energy boost.

Reaching the top

Steve Redgrave, world-class rower and gold medalist in five Olympics, was diagnosed with type 2 diabetes in 1998. Every day he takes five or six injections of fast-acting insulin to cope with his intense training. He eats snacks between training sessions and takes glucose tablets or a drink whenever he feels he needs a boost. He checks his blood sugar levels six or seven times daily.

"It's an advantage being a sportsman. You have to be very disciplined about your whole lifestyle. Diabetes is just another part of the equation. It's a pain in the neck, but that's all really."

STEVE REDGRAVE

People with diabetes need extra sugar during exercise, like all marathon runners.

After exercise

Most attacks of low blood sugar happen after exercise, so people with diabetes should eat a snack and test their blood sugar level when they finish.

Did you know?

- Footballers who have diabetes often take a glucose drink before a game, and at half-time.
- People with diabetes should always carry something like a banana or cereal bar around with them in case they do any unplanned exercise.
- A person with diabetes should always tell a coach or lifeguard about their condition.

Diabetes at home

Diabetes affects the whole family. When a child is first diagnosed with the condition, injections, blood tests, and planning a diet can take hours. Sometimes brothers and sisters feel left out.

Feeling jealous

A child who has just been diagnosed with diabetes becomes the center of attention. Life revolves around blood tests, injections, and the food they eat. Other children in the family may not envy the injections, but they can still feel jealous of the attention.

It's easy for a child to feel left out when their brother or sister has diabetes.

On the other hand, children with diabetes may be upset that they have to cope with the condition when their brothers and sisters don't. It's important for the family to talk through these problems. This can help to keep everyone happy.

"Sometimes I get really upset when I see my brother and sister eating candies whenever they want, because I feel I'm missing out."

LOUISA, AGE 13

When a child is first diagnosed with diabetes, injections can be difficult and take a long time.

Exercise is good for people with diabetes—and for the rest of the family, too.

Support groups

Parents of children with diabetes often join support groups. Here they talk to other people who are dealing with diabetes. This helps them to feel less isolated and more confident that they can cope.

Being positive

Diabetes isn't all bad. It can have a positive effect on family life by encouraging everybody to eat a healthier diet and exercise more often. The first months after diagnosis can be difficult, but a family soon learns to cope and in time may treat diabetes as nothing special.

Did you know?

- Brothers and sisters soon learn how to treat low blood sugar.
- Teenagers with diabetes may refuse to check their blood as a rebellion against the condition.
- In families where someone has diabetes, candies and chocolates often cause arguments. Children with diabetes can't always eat them as often as they would like.

When someone has diabetes, it can lead to healthier mealtimes for the whole family.

Diabetes at school

Anyone who looks after children needs to understand about diabetes. This is very important at school, where all children want to feel one of the crowd and just live a normal life.

All children with diabetes need a healthy meal in the middle of the day.

Talking to teachers

When a child is diagnosed with diabetes, or when a child with diabetes joins a school, their parents should meet the principal and class teacher. They need to discuss matters like the need for regular snacks, the risk of black outs, and preparing for gym or PE.

Children with diabetes can enjoy gym or PE so long as they eat a snack first.

School action

The parents of a child with diabetes may ask a school to make a plan for dealing with their child's condition. It helps if the school informs every member of staff, too. Children who do their own injections need a private place, as well as a supply of fast-acting carbohydrates available at all times. Teachers need to tell other pupils about diabetes, and explain the need for snacks.

Children with diabetes can enjoy school trips, which are an important part of school life.

Vacation fun

Children with diabetes can go on specially-run vacations where they try out new activities like canoeing, sailing, and windsurfing. This gives them the chance to have a break from home, make new friends, and share common experiences. It makes them realize they're not the only ones with diabetes and can help them to become more confident.

Activity vacations are a good way for children with diabetes to make new friends.

School trips

Children with diabetes do not need special attention. They take part fully in school activities, including sport and PE. School trips need a little extra planning. A teacher should always carry a spare injection kit and take extra food in case of delays. Children who give themselves injections can go on overnight trips.

"I was really dreading going back to school after my diagnosis. I knew that all my friends and teachers would be fussing over me, and I was right. It was 'Should you be eating that?' or 'Are you feeling OK?' It drove me mad."
TOM, AGE 13

Questions people ask

Can I drive if I have diabetes?
Yes, but there may be some restrictions. If a person has hypoglycemia, they could black out behind the wheel.

Will there ever be a cure for diabetes?
Maybe. Scientists are looking at ways to **transplant** healthy insulin-producing cells from one person to another. Or they may be able to make artificial ones.

Diabetes does not prevent people from driving a car.

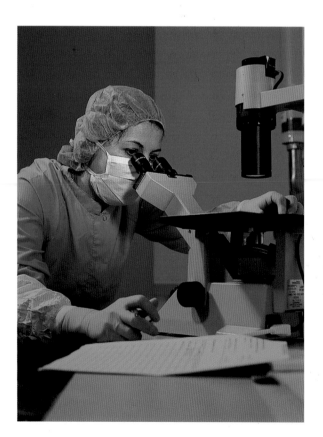

Are there any jobs I won't be able to do?
If you take insulin for diabetes, there may be some jobs you won't be able to do, such as working in the armed forces. Until 1999, there was a ban on people who take insulin for their diabetes being pilots in the U.S., but this has now changed.

Scientists are doing a great deal of research into diabetes. One day they may find a cure.

Some children inject themselves, but others want the help of a parent.

How old do you have to be to give yourself injections?

There is no special age. Some children, usually aged about ten and over, prefer to give themselves injections. Others prefer a parent to give them the injection.

Can I continue with my favorite sport now that I've got diabetes?

Definitely. Olympic rower Steve Redgrave does, but there may be some restrictions, for your safety. If you plan to ski, go climbing, or swim in the sea, it's wise to do this with a friend.

People with diabetes should always swim with a friend, in case they black out.

Can diabetes make people blind?

People who have diabetes sometimes have problems with their eyes. Usually, eye damage can be prevented by checking blood sugar levels every day and keeping them as normal as possible. Annual eye check-ups are important so that any problems can be treated early.

Glossary

bloodstream The flow of blood around the body.

blood vessel A tube that carries blood around the body.

carbohydrate An important source of energy that is found in starchy or sugary foods such as potatoes, rice, bread, pasta, candies, and cookies.

cell One of the billions of tiny building blocks that make up a plant or animal.

diabetologist A doctor who is specially trained to treat diabetes patients.

diagnose To discover what type of illness a person has.

dietician Someone who is an expert on food and how it affects the body.

dose The amount of medicine given to a patient.

fiber A bulky material that our bodies can't digest. It is found in foods like brown rice, wholemeal bread, and vegetables. Fiber helps keep the digestive system healthy.

gland An organ that produces substances which are used for certain jobs inside the body, such as digesting food.

glucose A type of sugar in the food we eat which we then burn as fuel.

heart attack A blockage in one of the arteries, or tubes, which supply blood to the heart. Without blood, parts of the heart muscle may stop pumping and die.

hyperglycemia A higher than normal amount of sugar in the blood. Someone with hyperglycemia feels thirsty and has to keep going to the bathroom. They also feel tired and begin to lose weight.

hypoglycemia A lower than normal amount of sugar in the blood. Someone with this may look pale, feel dizzy, have a headache, or start to sweat. They may also lose their temper suddenly or find it hard to concentrate.

insulin A chemical made by a gland called the pancreas. It controls the level of sugar in the blood.

kidney One of the two organs that take waste substances from the blood and turn them into urine.

nutrition The study of foods needed by the body to work properly.

pancreas A gland near the stomach that produces insulin, as well as juices to digest food.

plantain A tropical fruit, like a large banana with a green skin.

starchy Containing much starch— a white, powdery carbohydrate that has no taste or smell. Starchy foods include bread, tortillas, plantain, potatoes, pasta, cereals, and rice.

symptom One of the signs of a disease. A strong thirst is a symptom of diabetes, for example.

syringe A tool that is used to take samples of blood and to inject substances into the body.

tortilla A thin, flat, round cake of cornmeal.

transplant To remove an organ from an animal or a person and replace it with another.

unconscious Asleep or unaware.

urine The yellow waste liquid that leaves our bodies when we go to the bathroom.

Useful organizations

Here are some organizations you can contact for more information about diabetes:

American Diabetes Association
1701 North Beauregard St
Alexandria, VA 22311

Tel: (800) 342 2383
www.diabetes.org

Juvenile Diabetes Foundation International
120 Wall St, New York, NY 10005

email: info@jdfcure.org

Index